Who Moved My Cape?!

Letting Go of your
Superwoman Expectations

TRACY RICHARDSON, PH.D.

Who Moved My Cape?!
Letting Go of Your Superwoman Expectations

© Tracy Richardson, 2019
All Rights Reserved

Published by
Tracy Richardson Music
Terre Haute, IN

www.TracyRichardsonMusic.com

ISBN: 978-1-7923-2652-3

Printed in the United States by IngramSpark

Cover art by Bryan Bromstrup
www.Bbromart.com

Photos: Tracy Richardson
Author Photo: Lori Collings

superwoman syndrome[1]

a set of characteristics found in a woman who performs or attempts
to perform all the duties typically associated with several different
full-time roles, such as wage earner, mother, homemaker, and wife
(American Psychological Association, 2019).

Disclaimer: The contents of this book are not intended to replace
professional help when needed. If you are experiencing physical and/
or mental health struggles please seek appropriate professional help.

---

[1]   Superwoman Syndrome: https://dictionary.apa.org/superwoman-syndrome

For my mom ... the original superwoman in my life,
Delores Cunningham Collings, and all the superwomen I know.

• • • • •

This is a book for all women, with a special shout out to moms.
Moms are often *required* to be superwomen. Moms have to do
many things we are not ready for, things that require us to be much
stronger/wiser/faster/smarter than we thought we could be...

Things that call for a big-ass cape.

• • • • •

Special thanks...
Amanda Colleen Williams and *Songpreneurs* Songwriting and
Business Community for consistently encouraging me to keep
writing and to publish this book.

Katie Dailey, Sherry Schnake, Sharon Boyle, and Elizabeth Collins
for proofing and editing, and for being wonderful friends.

Superwoman Blues

Tracy Richardson, © 2016 Bridgeton Raccoons Music

Woke up this mornin', 'bout 6am
Woke up the kids, took care of them
Got myself ready, kissed my man goodbye
One mission accomplished now I'm on the fly

I need a cape, and some real comfy shoes
Cause every single day, I got the Superwoman Blues

I got to work, thousand things to do
I made a list...made coffee too
But that phone kept a-ringin', wouldn't leave me alone
I turned around and it was time to go

I need a cape, and some superpowers too
Cause every single day, I got the Superwoman Blues

Rolled in the drive, 'bout quarter to 6
Gotta help with the homework, Got dinner to fix
Five loads of laundry, gotta pay the bills
Don't know how much longer I can handle these thrills

I need a cape, and a phone booth too
Cause every single day, I got the Superwoman Blues

Yeah, I need a cape, and an Extra-Strength Tylenol too
Cause every single day.... I got the Superwoman... Blues

Preface

The first album I ever owned was *I am Woman*[2] by Helen Reddy. It was my 10th birthday; I got that record and a Mattel (or maybe Fisher Price?) portable record player. I loved the message of the title song: "I am woman, hear me roar, in numbers too big to ignore.... If I have to, I can do anything... I am strong, I am invincible, I am WOMAN...." I truly felt there was nothing I could not do, and the women who were writing and singing pop music in the 70s were reinforcing that message in the songs I listened to.

And let's face it. Modern society[3] is telling girls and women that we can do it all and have it all. We can be full time career women with husbands and children, and be the President of the PTA, and make homemade brownies for the Girl Scouts troop we are leading, and start our own business while looking like supermodels...And we believe those **lies**[4].

Early on I learned I was good at juggling a lot of things and *looking like* I was keeping it all together. I was literally trying to "do it all" before I even had my 16th birthday. I was gathering the material for my cape...

---

2   *I Am Woman*, by Helen Reddy and Ray Burton, © 1971 Universal Music Publishing

3   In speaking of "society" or "culture" in this book I am specifically referencing *American* society over the past 120 years or so. Societal views regarding women vary greatly across the globe and across time.

4   I use the term "lie" to describe cultural messages that seem *intended to deceive* as well as those that, in my opinion, are *simply not true*.

already a superwoman-wannabe.

Now, after more than a few years of trying to do it all, I'm figuring this out: It's time to stop trying to be a superwoman. It's ok to be mortal (flying is great once and a while and everyone should have some of those "highs" but we should never forget that gravity WILL eventually have its way). I'm also figuring out that maybe some of those things I've heard and believed as *facts* about my life as a woman are not really true!

So, my message to myself and to you throughout this book is this: **Give yourself permission to simply be the glorious, grounded, fully-human person that you are. Flaws and all. Ditch the toxic, cultural lies and replace them with healthy messages.**

Each chapter ends with a *Golden Nugget*[5]. These are things I wish I would have known as I went through the life experiences in that chapter. These are life-lessons that I hope will be of some help to you.

How to read this book:

Read it any way you want. No need to read the "chapters" in order. Skim the Table of Contents and find something that speaks to you. Start by reading that chapter and working through the exercises. It's your book and your process and your life, so read one chapter a month or sit down and read the whole thing start to finish (oh wait! You are a superwoman, so you will NEVER have time to do that!)

---

5   Golden Nugget: When I started teaching I would tell students at the end of class if they could remember nothing else about today's class, remember the "golden nugget."

Contents

I need to fit in with and impress others.   1

Getting enough sleep is a luxury.   5

My dreams and passions are not that important.   9

I probably won't succeed...why even try?   13

I have to do everything WELL...
    and make homemade peanut butter.   17

I'm a fraud... and people are going to find out.   21

My "life "can wait.   25

I don't really need to carve out time with friends.   29

I need to take care of everyone else's needs
    before I take care of mine.   33

I have too much to do to take a break.   37

If I'm different from others, I'm the one who needs to change.   41

I have to be available to everyone all the time.   45

Another life transition? Bring it on...I can take it. No biggie.   49

There is nothing special about me; anyone can do what I do.   53

I need to be productive 24/7.   57

I don't need to focus on me; that can wait.   59

I need to be on the same path as the women I admire.   63

I'm always busy, but I'm not accomplishing anything.   67

If I were younger/thinner/more attractive I'd be happy.   71

I'm stuck with a life I'm not excited about.   77

I'm too old to _____.   81

I need to speak/ act/ look "like a lady."   85

Who Moved My Cape?!

*Letting Go of your
Superwoman Expectations*

Lie:

I need to fit in with and impress others.

Truth:

Discover who YOU are and embrace it.

I won the spitting contest at the county fair.

No, not watermelon seed spitting....*tobacco* spitting.

My all-girl 4-H club dared me to enter the contest. No girl had ever done this, not even my friend Lisa who was tougher than 10 boys rolled into one. Of course, I said yes... I mean, I had to show everybody (and myself) that girls can do anything boys can do. I had to *impress* everyone.

I grew up with two older brothers and I always wanted to do everything they did and impress them. I thought they were the coolest. They, in turn, thought I was a spoiled brat (ok, ok, I was the only girl in the bunch, so MAYBE there was a tiny kernel of truth there).

When I was about 12 I asked them if I could try some of their *snuff* (translation: tobacco). Before you get entirely grossed out (or die from laughing if you are trying to picture me doing this) in the 70s it was very common for farm kids to use snuff, or "dip" ...and it was not illegal way back then. It's still pretty common even though we now know how dangerous it can be.

They eagerly complied with my request. I'm pretty sure they knew what would happen next. I got violently ill. But that didn't stop me from continuing to "chew" because I was so determined to be as tough as the boys and to impress them.

Back to the contest....

Spitting Contest, 1979

I showed up that night in the *Cow Palace*. (Side bar: The Cow Palace had a big arena at one end, where the livestock show was held, and a big stage at the other end, for the queen pageant, of course). There were about 10 guys and me in the contest.

Long story short, I won the contest. Well, just between you and me, I *actually* came in second, but they put my name and picture on the front of the county newspaper the next day (because, you know, it was such a historical event), so everyone in Parke County thinks I won even though a guy actually won (sorry, man!).

One of the guys in the contest was my boyfriend. As they say, if you beat your boyfriend in a tobacco spitting contest, you might be a redneck...

Three years later I stood on stage in that same Cow Palace for the fair queen contest. It was down to one other girl and me. The announcer said "Your 1982 Parke County Fair Queen is the former tobacco spitting champion, Tracy Collings!"

Fair Queen, 1982

Another time I wanted to ride my brother Brian's motorcycle to impress my cousins. We got into a huge fight because he wouldn't let me ride it. I'll summarize here to save me from reliving the trauma...I called him a *very bad* name while I was in earshot of my mom. It didn't end so well for me that day. In the words of Forrest Gump, "That's all I have to say about that".

Why was I always so eager to impress other people? To try and be someone I was not?

Part of wanting to impress is natural. Social psychology tells us humans have a strong need to "belong." Abraham Maslow put it in the center of his *Hierarchy of Needs*[6]. The need for emotional relationships drives human behavior.

Another part of wanting to impress is developmental. When you are a kid; you are *trying on* different personas to see what fits you, what feels right.

As you get into your 20s and 30s you should KNOW who you are and stop trying to impress, right? Not necessarily. And where does it stop? In the words of the great philosopher Will Smith "Too many people spend money they haven't earned to buy things they don't want to impress people they don't like."

I've heard several mature women (around the 50th birthday) say that there is a freedom and authenticity that comes with this middle age territory. One woman said "I turned 50 and now, *finally*, I simply don't care about what others think any more....and it is wonderful. I am who I am, and I don't give a thought to what others think of me anymore."

I'm over 50 and I'm beginning to understand. After all this time, I'm

6   Hierarchy of Needs: https://www.verywellmind.com/what-is-maslows-hierarchy-of-needs-4136760

finally realizing it's just too much work to try to impress someone else. I'm working on impressing myself.

Golden Nugget:

You are who you are, and you should be no one else. Don't waste your time trying to impress other people or trying to fit in with some group you don't really want to be part of, trying to be who you think THEY want you to be. Who knows...they may be trying to impress you!

Exercise:

Spend a few minutes writing down words and phrases that describe you. Think about the roles you play, adjectives that describe you, things you love to do, place you like to go, foods you love. On the back side of the paper, list those things that are NOT you.

Then spend 10 minutes using those words and phrases to write a description of YOU in third person, as if you were writing a story where you are introducing the reader to the character of "you." Make it a rich, detailed description. Mine might start like this:

> Tracy is a woman in her 50s who loves music. Everything music. Many kinds of music. She loves to write songs, play piano, and sing and has been doing that since she was about 10. She is strong. She has weathered a lot of storms, raised 3 kids, and takes care of her husband who has a disability. She is an extremely hard worker; don't tell her something cannot be done or she will prove you wrong. She LOVES strong coffee, dark chocolate, and too many desserts to name. She does not like liver, sauerkraut, cruelty, or arrogance. She cannot stand to see kids suffer. She likes to help and encourage people. She adores traveling, being active, spending time in nature (if she has a lot of bug spray), and feeling the sun on her face any time of year. She is not perfect and she is a work in progress.

Post your self-description on your bathroom mirror. Read it out loud each morning. It's a good start to remind you of who you truly are.

Lie:

Getting enough sleep is a luxury.

Truth:

Your sleep is essential.

I'm an early riser. I think I always have been. I remember as a kid my dad would be outside by about 7:30am starting up the tractor...I'm a light sleeper so there was no going back to sleep after that kind of "alarm clock."

My colleague and friend Sharon, who is often my roommate when we go to professional conferences, says that when my alarm goes off I literally jump out of bed, raring to go. I can't say that every day is like that, but there is something special about the morning. It is fresh and new and full of hope and, at least for a little while, it feels like anything is possible, like I felt as a kid.

Yes... I was the weird kid who was the first to go to sleep at a slumber party (therefore I always was the object of the other girls' pranks, like putting my bra outside to freeze or putting mascara and toothpaste in my hair). I got up early even on weekends. I still do.

But oh my gosh, afternoons are BRUTAL! I'm always tired in the afternoon. I really think there is something to be said for taking an afternoon nap because if I take one...even just 10 minutes....I awake feeling completely refreshed. But I don't often have that luxury.

In 5th grade my teacher, Mrs. Cash, would read to the class after lunch. She turned out the lights, and told us to put our heads down and rest as we listened. Wow...no way that would fly today! After she finished reading we had to draw a picture of the story we heard. And even sleepyhead-me would not truly fall asleep; I just got very relaxed.

The story she was reading (I distinctly remember "The Hobbit") would come to life in front of me. I remember drawing a hobbit up in a tree after one of those reading experiences. What a beautiful way to teach us great literature, to feed our imaginations, and to allow us to even rest a bit!

In high school, I remember having Mr. Brooks' chemistry class right after lunch. Oh gosh, that was torture! His voice was very monotone and it was tough to stay interested. I was a good student but I couldn't force myself to stay awake. I'm ashamed to say sometimes my friends and I would sniff Vick's VapoRub inhalers to try to stay awake. It never worked.

Throughout college, I often *had* to take an afternoon nap because I got up early for classes and played keyboards in a band until 1-2am. A quick nap was a survival skill.

As grown women with 1000x the responsibilities we had in young adulthood, I think we sometimes put even our basic need for sleep on the backburner. I know...I've been there, done that (doing that still sometimes). "I just need to get one last load of laundry folded....I just need to pack lunches and then I'll go to bed...hey that furnace filter looks awfully dirty, so I'd better just cha..."

Enough...go to bed!

Naps are fine but a better plan is to get a good night's sleep. The

National Sleep Foundation (NSF, 2019) states most people need 7-9 hours of quality sleep per night, but women get only about 6.5 on average. Women can also have trouble sleeping due to hormone changes that accompany their monthly cycle, pregnancy, and menopause. (It is so fun to be a woman sometimes).

Also, according to the NSF[7], women tend to multi-task throughout the day and *use more of their actual brains* than men (I swear I'm not making this up!). This leads to a greater need for quality sleep (the more you use your brain during the day, the more it needs to rest while asleep). This is all making me (yawn!) a little tired, so I think I'll turn in.

Golden Nugget:

Know your body's rhythms and do your best to prioritize quality and quantity of sleep. You may need to turn in earlier, or use ear plugs if you have a partner who snores. You may need to adjust your bedtime through the work week so you CAN wake up early those days that require it. And maybe let yourself sleep in a bit on Saturdays.

(PS.... I still sneak a quick nap on my desk once in a while. Don't tell the teacher...)

Exercise:

Sometimes we are not really aware of how little we are sleeping. Keeping a sleep journal is a good first step toward improving your sleep habits. Any old notebook or pad of paper will do. You can track a lot of things in a sleep journal, or you can keep it simple. My suggestion is to keep it simple at first; you can always add other information later.

Once you have kept the journal for 3-4 weeks, you may start to see patterns emerge (for example, maybe you notice that you don't sleep well on Friday nights). You can use the information from your journal to perhaps solve why that is happening. Maybe you overdid it on alcohol on those Friday nights.

---

7   NSF: https://www.sleepfoundation.org/articles/do-women-need-more-sleep-men
https://www.sleepfoundation.org/articles/women-and-sleep

You can also do some reading about things that often interfere with sleep: alcohol, caffeine, certain medications, use of phone/iPad/TV before bedtime, and not having a consistent bedtime routine are just a few of the culprits!

	Sun. (Date)	Mon. (Date)	Tue. (Date)	Wed. (Date)	Thur. (Date)	Fri. (Date)	Sat. (Date)
Time I went to sleep last night							
Time I awoke this morning							
Total hours of sleep last night							
Notes (reasons I may have slept the amount I did last night)							

Once you get used to doing the journal you might add rows for these activities:

- Number of caffeinated drinks I had yesterday
- Number of alcoholic drinks I had yesterday
- Naps
- Stressors

There is a good example of a free sleep journal from the Sleep Foundation[8] you can copy for your use!

---

8   Sleep Diary: https://www.sleepfoundation.org/sites/default/files/inline-files/SleepDiaryv6.pdf

Lie:

My dreams and passions are not that important.

Truth:

Your dreams and passions make you who you are.

When I was about seven I remember my Grandpa putting me on his lap when he played his old upright piano. He had never had a lesson, but could play a few little ditties by ear. I later found out he had a brother who would hear a song and then could just play it note for note. I loved putting my hands on grandpa's and pretending it was me making those beautiful sounds as he played.

In church, we had a wonderful lady who played the piano and taught us kids various songs that we would then sing for the congregation. I loved watching Mary Peffley play that old, out of tune piano. Her hands would just fly! And I loved (and still love) those old hymns like *The Church in the Wildwood, In the Garden,* and *Mansion Over the Hilltop.* I enjoyed picking out the harmonies, even though I didn't know that is what they were called.

When I turned nine I asked for a piano and my parents got me a Kimball upright. I remember the day the delivery truck arrived; they had trouble finding our house out in the middle of nowhere. It seemed to take forever as they pulled into our front yard to get close enough to the house to unload it.

My mom knew I had this intense love for music. She still tells stories of me singing "Oh Christmas Tree" in front of our tree when I was three. When that piano arrived at our house I was screaming with excitement. The one thing she said that I'll never forget was "You can do and be anything you want; if you want to study in Vienna, I'll make it happen." (Yeah... I have the best mom ever). I will never forget that.

I started lessons with Mrs. Mary Brown right away. I LOVED playing! However, I did not love practicing the *written* music. Mrs. Brown was always telling me to practice more. So that meant every Saturday morning, before the lesson, I was "cramming" (not an effective way to develop your music skills!). What I really loved was to play by ear, especially after I learned how to do some of the basics.

I learned a lot from those lessons and from sticking with it. Once, I entered a talent contest where I was going to play "The Entertainer" by Scott Joplin. I had to start over three times because of forgetting the next part, but I did NOT run off stage (I think stubbornness and perseverance are two sides of the same coin). I learned I could do it, I could accomplish a goal, and I could remain on a stage even when the heat was on. So what if I got 3rd place out of 4 contestants? Who cares?! I hung in there.

I started writing songs by about age 10...songs about clouds and cows and just whatever I saw in the world around me. When my dad would move the cattle from one pasture to another, he would tell me to wait at the new pasture. When the cattle came down the road my job was to stand in the middle of the road and "shoo" them in through the gate to the new pasture. Because they moved pretty slowly down the road

I had about an hour to kill, so I would just make up songs. I also loved sitting by our pond and being in nature. It made me think big thoughts and have a respect and reverence for nature. It fed my songwriting (it still does!).

Dad told me many times over the years that he remembers being inside the house, taking off his boots or sitting and reading the paper, and I would burst in and run past him to get to the piano because I had a song idea. I needed to figure it out and write it down before it slipped away.

When I was about 12 I got the sheet music for *Desperado*[9]. I already knew I loved it because I'd heard it on the radio so I was super motivated to learn that music. And I did. I ended up playing Desperado hundreds of times, at my mom's request, for every living soul who had the misfortune of coming in our house. Years later, I sang it on stage in front of about 8,000 people when the band I was in (the Don Morris Band) opened for George Strait. Then a few years later I was fortunate enough to record that song and put it on a CD so my mom could hear it anytime. It is still one of my favorites to play and sing.

I started playing for weddings when I was 15. That was huge. I felt honored to be asked, but also an enormous pressure to do a good job. I mean, this is a wedding! The couple will remember this day forever! Doing a good job gave me confidence and helped spur my desire to do more with music.

Also at 15 I started playing in bar bands. Now, dear friends, I could write an entire book about those adventures. But in the interest of time and preserving my reputation I'll just say that playing in those bands did several things for me. First, it really helped me develop as a musician. I became better at playing the keyboard, developed my ear, gained the ability to listen carefully, and learned to "give and take" in the music. Second it taught me a lot about human nature, especially when said humans are drinking to excess. You see a lot of things from the stage. Enough said!

---

9   *Desperado*, by Don Henley and Glenn Frey, ©1973 Cass County Music and Red Cloud Music

Music was everything to me; I never imagined doing any other career (well there was that short phase in junior high when I wanted to be a paleontologist. Although I did love dinosaurs, I think I liked 'paleontology' because it was a long word).

Golden Nugget:

Your passions are in you for a reason. In fact, your passions ARE you. Those interests combined with your DNA are unique to the world, and the world needs that combination.

Exercise:

Grab a pen and paper and write quick responses to this prompt:

If you were very wealthy, if you had no obligations to anyone, and you could do *anything* with your time, what would you do? How would you spend your days?

What are your passions? What do you love?

Lie:

I probably won't succeed...why even try?

Truth:

You don't KNOW until you try.

A few days before Christmas, when I was 14, my dad left home to go to a livestock show[10] or something like that.

I really don't remember where he went. I just remember that I thought it was completely unfair that he got to go on a trip and we had to be stuck at home in frozen Indiana. "We" meant my mom, my 5-year-old brother, and me (my older brothers were 20 and 22, so they were not around home much by then).

---

10   A livestock show is an event where the animals are led around an arena where they are judged for weight, muscle mass, etc.

I told my mom how completely unfair this situation was. Why did Dad get to go somewhere "exotic" and we had to stay home in the bleak Indiana winter? (In reality, he probably went to Oklahoma or somewhere like that, but the 14 year old mind likes to exaggerate).

I said "Why don't we go to Florida?! We have no reason to stay here. The weather would be nicer, and we could go to a beach" (I can be very convincing when I believe in something). My mom said "Well, that might be a great idea, but we could never get an affordable flight this close to Christmas."

Never say "never" to a teenage girl dreaming of warm ocean breezes and suntanned lifeguards.

I picked up the phone book (side bar: a "phone book" is an ancient artifact of 20th century American culture. It was a thick book with white pages and yellow pages. Companies' phone numbers were listed in the yellow pages. If you'd like to see one of these books, visit a library...oops, those are pretty scarce now, too). I looked for "Airlines" and found the number for one of the companies and made a call. They had 3 seats round trip to Tampa, and they were pretty cheap, too! Mom said "Ok! Let's do it!"

We booked the trip and booked it out of Indiana.

I'll never forget that trip. We rented a powder blue Thunderbird; they were out of economy cars (shoot!), but gave us the economy price (score!). I felt so...free. Traveling does that for me...it energizes me and makes me temporarily feel like I can do anything. While we were there we visited some of my parents' friends and spent a lot of time by the pool and beach.

And I like to think we looked really cool driving around in a T-Bird!

I remember feeling so ...empowered! I had really wanted something that seemed completely out of the question, but I pursued it and found out that it really was possible (thank you, Mom). I think that was an important life lesson for me. You don't know if you don't try.

It was the most amazing Christmas...ever!

I've had other examples of this...times when I had to decide to *go for it* (even though "it" was something big) or to *throw in the towel* before

I even tried. And yes, many times I gave up before I should have, like when I really wanted a particular job but did not apply.

There are many reasons women sometimes don't even try for that thing they want, especially when it comes to work situations.

One widely-cited reason is the so-called "confidence gap"[11] and it goes something like this:

> *Women don't apply for jobs unless they are 100% qualified, whereas a man will apply if he is only 60% qualified.*

This study has been cited by a lot of authors in support of the theory that women have less confidence than men.

However, the study has not been replicated (which is an important step in scientific investigation). AND the original study (by Hewlett Packard) cannot even be located! Soooo... maybe it's not about a "confidence gap."

Many researchers, authors, and bloggers are now looking a little deeper and finding out that it's more about how women are *viewed* when they *go for it*. It appears that men who apply for jobs for which they are qualified, AND show confidence, are likely to be hired. However, women who apply for jobs for which they are qualified, must show a *mix* of confidence and *humility* in order to be considered. **Women have to balance their confidence with stereotypically feminine traits like empathy and altruism.**

Not fair. Not fair at all. But as they say, "it is what it is".

Until gender stereotypes go away, at least we now know the rules of the game. Just because I, as a woman, may have *extra* hoops to jump through, it's not going to stop me from going for something I really want.

Golden nugget:

Listen to your heart. Don't let anything, including lack of confidence, or fear, or twisted rules, stand in your way of what you want. When you really want something, when you feel in your gut that that something is *good*....go for it. Use your own creative mix of confidence and whatever

---

11   The "confidence gap": https://www.theatlantic.com/family/archive/2018/09/women-workplace-confidence-gap/570772/

else it takes. The worst thing that can happen is you get a "no" or that you may be viewed negatively by *some* people for having "thought so highly" of yourself as to try for this big thing.

But what does their viewpoint really matter in the grand scheme of your life? Nada.

And at least you will not have thrown in the towel[12] before the game even started!

(And that's the end of my sports metaphors...)

Exercise:

Grab a notebook and pen[13], then find a quiet place to sit and quiet your mind for a few minutes. Consider these questions (and write down your honest answers):

1. *What have I done in my life that was really difficult?* (Raised a child? Started a new job? Made it through a rough patch in a relationship? Moved to a new place?)
2. *What factors helped me to do it?* (Determination? Support from others? Stubbornness? Work ethic?)
3. *What do I want with all my heart and soul, but have not allowed myself to go after?* (Don't hold back, now. Be honest).
4. *What is holding me back?*
5. *What steps do I need to take help me attain that desire?*

Now draw a set of stairs on the paper, starting in the bottom left corner and going diagonally to the upper right corner. Draw you (stick person is fine) at the bottom, and label your goal/desire at the top. Label each stair with the steps you need to take to get to your goal. Once you label the steps, put dates under each one to help give you a timeframe to work with.

It sounds simple, perhaps. But *visualizing* your goal and how to get there can help it happen.

---

12   Origin of the term "throwing in the towel": https://www.phrases.org.uk/meanings/throw-in-the-towel.html

13   I prefer pencil and paper because it makes me think and process differently than if I type. But use whatever method works for you!

ie:

I have to do everything WELL...
and make homemade peanut butter.

Truth:

You're going to fail at lots of things.
And Jif is perfectly fine.

I had my first child at age 27. Even though I was working part time I craved times with other adults.

So about once a week one of the young moms in my friend group would host a play date; we would all go to one of our houses so the kids could play and (theoretically) we adults could talk.

Great plan... except it rarely worked out so neatly. Some child would always get hurt, or want the toy someone else was playing with.

At one gathering, we moms were in the kitchen getting lunch ready for the kids. The host mom that day began to talk about the HOMEMADE peanut butter she was putting on her child's sandwich. She *made* the baby food from scratch when her daughter was a baby and in fact made most of the child's foods from scratch.

I was amazed. I had never even heard of homemade peanut butter. I thought Jif, Peter Pan, and Skippy made all the peanut butter in the world.

She talked about how much healthier it was for her child and, because she cared so much about her child's health, she could not feed her store-bought stuff. And there seemed to be an implicit message: I, too, *should* be making my child's food.

I felt shamed. Did I not care about my child enough?

(Sidebar: when you hear someone say, or imply, that you "should" be doing this or that, proceed with caution. Some people just really like to make others feel bad so they feel more superior.)

Back to the homemade peanut butter.

What? Honestly, if someone wants to make their own baby food, I applaud them, but no one should heap guilt on others for making different choices. I was just trying to figure out how to get five minutes of uninterrupted sleep and get to work with shoes that matched. There was no way I was going to try to make peanut butter from scratch.

Over the next few years I had another child, began working full time again (teaching at a small college), got my master's degree, wrote really long reports at work, had a third child, got my doctorate, and became chair of my department. Easy cheesy, right? (heh heh ....that's sarcasm).

I didn't sleep much.

When my babies were little I remember hearing "experts" on Oprah, or in People magazine, or somewhere, say "You have to get your baby on a schedule, so even if it seems counterintuitive, if it is time for your baby to eat, wake her up."

My response to that was something casual like "YOU HAVE GOT TO BE FREAKING KIDDING ME!!! I HAVE NOT SLEPT SINCE THE DAY THIS BABY WAS BORN, SO WHEN THIS CHILD SLEEPS I'M SLEEPING TOO AND THERE AIN'T NO WAY IN HELL I'M WAKING HER UP!!"

I stand by this rule...never wake a sleeping child unless the house is on fire.

And as long as Jif is still in business, I'm <u>not</u> making homemade peanut butter!

Golden Nugget:

Refuse to let others make you feel guilty for anything. Remember Eleanor Roosevelt's quote: "No one can make you feel inferior without your consent."

You are doing the best you can with the resources you have. Repeat that out loud: "I am doing the best I can with the resources I have."

Exercise:

Make a list of hurtful "shoulds" you have had directed toward you. Then write briefly how you handled each one. How would you want to handle it if it happened again? How would your best friend respond and defend you if s/he heard someone saying that hurtful thing to you? Sometimes we can learn from those who love us how to stick up for ourselves.

Lie:

I'm a fraud...
and people are going to find out.

Truth:

You are the real deal.

When I started teaching college courses in music therapy I was 29 years old, pregnant with my second child, and completely unsure of why I was asked to teach. Yes, I had been a very good student and I was a music therapist. But what the heck did I know about *teaching* music therapy??

I had NEVER thought of myself as teacher material (well, not since I was a kid and I would play "school" with my friends). I did not even have a master's degree (gasp!) at the time.

I found out after one semester that the students seemed to be learning what they needed to learn, and I enjoyed it. I liked feeling like I was helping "bring up" the next generation of music therapists. But I also felt like an imposter.

In fact, this is a common phenomenon called "Imposter Syndrome[14]." It is not a mental illness, but it is recognized by helping professionals as a serious form of self-doubt that many people deal with, especially when they are starting some new endeavor.

It's not just wondering "Do I have all the right skills to do this job?" It is more about wondering "Do I belong here?" and "When will they find out I don't really know what I'm doing?" You often spend tremendous amounts of time on projects because you want to make SURE they are done well. And, when they ARE done well, you chalk it up to sheer luck, and the fear of being "found out" can intensify. It can cause anxiety and depression.

Imposter (or fraud) syndrome was originally thought to apply only to women (and it IS very common in women), but eventually it was noticed in men as well. Many people who have this syndrome are perfectionists and over-achievers.

By the way, I also remember having this feeling when I became a mom. I mean, yes, I had just *birthed a child* so I knew I WAS a mom. But when I was leaving the hospital I felt like "Oh my gosh...I am responsible for a tiny, helpless, human being! Don't these people know I don't know what I'm doing??" Fortunately, I had lots of family and friends that helped out; it seems to be well-known that new parents need mentoring.

That is one of the keys: Find supportive, encouraging mentors. People who have been in your shoes and lived through it. People who will remind you of how much you actually DO know. As a young teacher, I had my colleagues to go to with questions and to give me a pep talk when I needed it.

As a young mom, I had my own mom, and friends who were moms, to call on. It made a world of difference. I found out I was not expected to know everything right away. Go figure.

You can also change your thinking and your self-talk. Changing your thinking can eventually change your behavior. For example, if you find

---

14   Imposter Syndrome: https://www.apa.org/gradpsych/2013/11/fraud

yourself thinking "This project needs to be perfect before I submit it", change that narrative to "I'm going to do my best on this project but I'm not going to let it consume me."

And self-talk is not just something that needs to happens in your head; it needs to happen out loud. You need to *hear* yourself saying a positive message like "Tracy, you can do this....it is not bigger than you." Over time, self-talk can actually change how you think, feel, and act.

The thing is every new experience brings new challenges. Everyone feels like a fish out of water once in a while. But if it is causing you anxiety, take some of those steps above.

You may be a *newbie*, but you are not an imposter or a fraud.

Golden Nugget:

Feeling like a fraud is an irrational (yet completely normal) fear that many people experience, especially when they are in a new job or facing a new challenge. Recognize it for what it is and don't accept it as reality.

Exercises:

1. Make a list of all the things you do well. Come on...be honest. Claim it. You might even ask other people to chime in. Then circle all the things on your list that you are utilizing in this new job or life experience. Interesting, huh? Your strengths are showing!
2. Look in the mirror and tell yourself this every morning: "You got this. You know more than you think you know! This thing is not bigger than you."
3. Recognize when you are being perfectionistic; change your expectations to "good enough."
4. Celebrate your achievements. When you finish that big "thing" reward yourself with something you enjoy (glass of wine, new music, avocado toast....oh, sorry, that is my list!)

Lie:

My life can wait.

Truth:

Your life is happening NOW... so live it.

I was up until 2 or 3am several nights in a row trying to finish a BIG report for work. A report than ended up being about 150 pages plus about a dozen appendices. So...much...fun (not). I was a zombie.

Accredited music schools have to do a thorough "self-study" every so often. It includes about a year's worth of gathering data and writing a **humongous** report stating how your institution is meeting all the standards. I was the lead person on our self-study and it was the biggest assignment I had ever tackled. And I did it (with help from my wonderful colleagues).

My kids were 4, 9, and 12. I was working full time, trying to juggle their schedules and keep up with household necessities like cooking and cleaning. (Ok, to be honest, the "cleaning" was put on a back burner for several years!). I was up early every day, making lunches, getting them and me ready, driving my son to preschool, going to work, trying to make it to my daughters' after-school dance classes and ball games, etc. I often felt I did more before 9:00 a.m. than I should have to do all day.

It was all about doing what HAD to be done and trying to make sure I was being a good mom. There seemed to be very little time for me. I imagine that even if the details of your story are different, you can relate.

And let's be real; there are definitely "seasons" in our lives where we are busier than others. But, looking back, I wish I had put more priority on carving out time for me (dark chocolate only goes so far). Time with friends, time for my songwriting.

Eventually I did find my way back to filling up MY cup. I got back to my music.

In 2011, I went to a local workshop held by a successful songwriter. That led to joining NSAI (Nashville Songwriters Association International) and going to a songwriting camp in Nashville. Then I started attending monthly NSAI meetings in Indianapolis which was a nice way to meet others in the songwriting community and to hear guest speakers who often came up from Nashville.

One of those guest speakers was a dynamic woman named Amanda Colleen Williams. I was immediately impressed with her accomplishments, passion, vision, and authenticity. I joined her songwriting and business community (Songpreneurs) in 2013 and started attending the annual conference. I met lots of other songwriters, started co-writing with some of them, and began to really dig into the craft and the business of songwriting.

There is a Bible verse that says there is a time for everything. A time to weep, a time to laugh. A time to mourn, a time to dance, and so on.

As I began to spend more time on my music again I felt like it was *time* for this. It was *my* time for music. It IS my time. I spent a lot of years doing very important, very worthwhile things...having babies, raising them well, going back to school, getting my career going, taking care of my family and job, etc. I am glad I did all those things.

But now it's time for me. And what "feeds" me is to dive into my music making. What feeds you? Are you nourished?

Golden Nugget:
Superwomen of the world, listen up...

There is a time you'll need to put on that cape and do *more than is humanly possible*. There are times you will feel like you are attending to everyone's needs *except* your own. Sometimes you may almost forget what it is that you want and need. But don't. Don't lose track of those things...the things *you* want and need. You want and need them for a reason. They make up who you are. When you pursue those passions, you *fill a hole* in you, which fills a hole in the world.

Exercise: Vision Board[15]

1. Write a list of goals and dreams you have. Be bold and honest. If you are not sure of exact goals, write words and phrases that represent your values, your desires, and passions.

2. Get a poster board, some old magazines and favorite photos (the printed-out kind), scissors, and a glue stick. Go on. I'll wait.

3. Now, grab those photos and magazines...find pictures and words that represent your goals and dreams, and things you love. Things that you gravitate toward. **Don't analyze it, don't question it. Just find things that attract you and cut them out.** Love to travel? Maybe cut out pictures of exotic beaches, or mountains. Love to write? Find pictures of books or journals. Make sure to include a photo of YOU ...one that shows you enjoying something, smiling. Start pasting the pictures on the board, however it makes sense to you.

---

15   Vision boards are sometimes associated with the "The Law of Attraction" which basically states that what you focus on will come to you. I'm not sure I buy into this 100% but I DO think that focusing on positive thoughts *can* sometimes help you feel more positive, and when you feel more positive you may be more likely to take action toward your goals.

4. Next, think about favorite sayings or quotes that you like. Write them in the white spaces of the board.

5. This is your vision board. It affirms who you are, what you love, and maybe can help you decide where you want to go next. When it is finished and you step back and look at it as a whole, you may learn something about yourself. You may learn there is some piece of you that has not been attended to, some passion you have not pursued, some vision you have for your life that you didn't previously see.

6. Put your vision board in a place where you'll see it every day. Spend time looking at it and pondering what it is 'telling' you. Looking at it often and thinking about the pictures and words may help you move toward your goals.

ie:

I don't REALLY need to carve out time with friends.

Truth:

Friends are a lifeline to your sanity.

All those years that I was having babies, running around with kids, going to work, going to graduate school, there was not a lot of time for nurturing friendships.

Or maybe I just did not prioritize it?

I think it was both. I had a small group of friends from church that sometimes went to a movie or to dinner, but it seems like those times were few and far between. And yes, we really cared about each other. But because we were *church* friends, part of me that felt I couldn't fully "let my hair down". I was trying to live up to who I thought I was supposed to be. We never stayed out late, never swore, and never even had a glass of wine together. Still, I loved (love) them deeply.

I have another group of friends that gets together a few times a year; we've been doing that for 30+ years. There are six couples; we refer to ourselves as "The Dockers Gang" because all the men seem to wear Dockers-style pants. The women are some of my best friends. However, it's hard to stay *connected* when you are working and raising babies and just doing everything that has to be done day to day. I know I can count on them for anything.

Things changed around 2011. My doctorate was done, my kids were older, and I had left the church I had gone to for 20 years. I made a new group of friends. I was becoming my own person; more assured of what I liked, needed, and wanted. More comfortable with who I was.

I rediscovered how utterly *healing* it is to be real and *uncensored* with other women. Women you trust and who won't judge you. Women who will tell (and laugh at) stupid, bawdy jokes. To (sometimes) drink a bit too much and to have friends who will drive you home. Friends for whom you will hold their hair back after they drink too much (Sorry for the graphic description, but I'm being real here). Women who allow you to be imperfect.

We can get so busy with living our lives and doing all the checklists that we forget about how important it is to spend time with friends.

I'm talking about real, uninterrupted time with friends…not "oh let's talk while the kids are playing on the playground". While that is better than nothing, most of your attention is (rightfully so) going to be on your kids… and not on connecting with your friend. And you will most definitely have interruptions.

You NEED friends. And they need you.

Golden Nugget:

My advice to those of you who might be just starting out in your career, or who are raising small children, or whatever…FIND GOOD FRIENDS. And spend time with them. Make it a priority. Have your significant other watch the kids once in a while, or get a baby sitter or another trusted adult. Leave work on time; that big project will still be there when you get back on Monday. Don't make work more important than you-time.

Exercise:

Down the left-hand side of a paper write qualities or descriptors you need in a friend at this point in your life (it can change based on the stage of life you are in). For example: Thoughtful, Non-judgmental, Will let me rant about my husband, Will go to chick flicks with me, Likes a glass of wine with dinner, Makes me laugh hysterically, etc. Write one item on each line. Then, next to each quality write the name of one (or more) of your friends who fits that description.

You might also approach it the other way around: List your friends down the left side of a paper, then beside each one, list what qualities you enjoy from your friendship with each person.

This is not meant as a tool to count who possesses the most "good" qualities; it is simply a self-awareness exercise. Hopefully it will help you become aware of both your needs and those friends that help you meet those needs.

Hint: you can extend this a little further and write down what qualities YOU bring to your friendships. Again, self-awareness is the first step in making your life what you want it to be.

Katie, Sherry, Beth, Sharon, Me

Lie:

I need to take care of everyone else's needs before I take care of mine.

Truth:

You can't help anyone if you are dead. (Don't be so dramatic, Tracy.)

Truth (Take 2):

You can't take care of anyone else when you are passed out on the floor.

My husband has MS...multiple sclerosis.

He was diagnosed at age 29, shortly before we got engaged. That was over 30 years ago.

I feel fortunate that in those early years of marriage he could still walk and work and do many "normal" activities. But he has (and we have) struggled with his physical limitations for our entire marriage. I'm not going to lie...it's been hard.

As I type, I know I need to head to the other room to help him get dressed. I'll be right back...

Thanks for waiting.

MS is a shitty disease. Well, I don't know any diseases or conditions that are pleasant. Cancer sucks, heart disease sucks, mental illness sucks, diabetes sucks (he also has diabetes due to many years of steroid treatments). All I know is that MS has robbed us of a lot of normalcy.

Stress causes MS to be worse, so he had to "retire" at age 36. When he started losing balance he began using a cane. Then, if we knew we would be walking a lot, we would take a wheelchair. Then he was using a wheelchair all the time, and a shower bench, a hospital bed, and a van with a ramp. Travel became very limited.

(RANT WARNING: Do you know how inaccessible the world STILL is in 2019? "ADA compliant" bathrooms are often NOT **functional** for someone in a wheelchair. If there's not enough room to transfer from the chair to the toilet, the grab bars don't help a bit! And do you have any idea how freaking hard it is to get a <u>truly</u> accessible hotel room?!)

On top of dealing with his illness I had all the "normal" craziness of life. Full time job, three kids, aging parents. I went to grad school when my babies were four and one; I went for my doctorate (with a third child) when they were 13, 10, and 5.

I'm not looking for sympathy; I want to make a point here. Even if you don't have a spouse or other significant person in your life with some sort of major challenge, life can be really hard and your own well-being can suffer. **When others depend on you it is all too easy to put your own self last** (hello, all you moms out there).

Every so often someone would say to me "What are you doing to take care of yourself?"

For years I had no idea what to say to that. I would hem and haw and say something like "Oh I'm fine, I do little things to take care of myself."

But I wasn't always fine. I had a lot on my shoulders. There were times I was really burned out and not coping well.

Fortunately, I have great friends. I have a wonderful husband who, even though he could not work or do lots of physical things around the house, became the *chauffeur* for our kids in all their activities. I have an exercise regimen that helps me feel good physically and mentally. Walks outside connect me to nature and fill me up spiritually.

And as the kids became more independent and began flying the coop, I took a deep dive into my passion, songwriting. It nurtures my soul. And that has been essential for my own well-being.

I am worth taking care of. And so are you.

Golden nugget:

You have to take care of YOU. It is not an option! It's *airplane logic*[16]... like the flight attendant tells you before takeoff: "If the cabin loses pressure, the oxygen masks will descend. Put your OWN mask on first before you attempt to help anyone else."

We can't help someone else if we are passed out on the floor.

Exercise:

Start with a list of the 6 areas of wellness[17] (I'll help you...they are listed below). In the first column, list ways you are attending to this area of your life. In the second column, brainstorm things that you could fairly easily do to begin nurturing this area. I've given you an example below:

	How I take care of myself...	How I can BETTER take care of myself
Emotional	Journal about my feelings	Talk to a friend about something I'm struggling with
Spiritual		
Occupational		
Social		
Physical		
Intellectual		

Think of that airplane story. The first column consists of the masks you already carry with you. The second column lists those masks you need to acquire! Emergencies will happen.

---

16   Thank you Amanda Colleen Williams for the metaphor

17   Six Dimensions of Wellness: https://www.nationalwellness.org/page/Six_Dimensions

Tracy and George, 2019

Lie:

I have too much to do to take a break.

Truth:

You will crash if you don't deliberately schedule downtime.

I get it. You have a lot on your plate.

There are only 24 hours in a day and you have 26 hours' worth of things that need to be done. You have to go to work, buy groceries, do the laundry, pay the bills, feed the cat, etc. Even if you are fortunate enough to have a life partner to share these duties with, it can be overwhelming.

Taking care of YOU can become the very lowest priority... the last thing on your to-do list.

We have all experienced a time when we pushed ourselves too hard for too long. What happens next? Often, we get sick. A cold or flu sets in, or some ache or pain gets worse. Our bodies are saying "ENOUGH!"

I teach at a college. Anyone who teaches is subject to a particular rhythm in their life. There is a beginning and end to each school year. There's a beginning and end to each semester (or quarter) and typically there is a break in between semesters. However, the "break" is often a time of intense preparation for the next semester.

For many teachers that rhythm is something like this: teach in the fall, take a brief winter break, teach in the spring, have a summer break, teach in the fall, etc. Lather, rinse, repeat.

But academia is changing, especially at the college/university level. Most colleges and universities are trying to attract more adult learners and so they offer online courses. They also offer those courses in different formats, such as offering an option of taking an 8-week course instead of a 16-week course.

There are also lots of *accelerated* programs popping up. For example, at our college you can get a certain graduate degree (36 credits) in one year. That's intense for both the student and the professors. Not much down time for anyone involved.

And let me just say, I realize EVERY job has its own rhythms and stresses. I'm talking about teaching because that's the world I've known for over two decades.

What I have noticed is that professors LIVE for those breaks (just as the students do). We run full throttle right up to that break. I often say that each semester is like a snowball rolling down a hill. It starts out small, rolling slowly and gently. As the semester progresses, the snowball gets larger and larger, rolls faster and faster, scoops up everything in its way, until it's a massive snow-boulder going 100 miles an hour then.... CRASH! It hits a tree at the bottom of the hill and explodes!

The long-awaited break arrives...and I'm in bed sick. My body has had it!

Golden Nugget:

Everything in nature has a rhythm...there is day followed by night followed by day, etc. There are seasons, each one with its own purposes. The tide comes in and goes out and the moon goes through different phases.

Our bodies and minds have a natural rhythm too; we require rest. Not just sleep, but REST. And our bodies and minds cannot wait until its convenient for us to take that break.

Exercises:

1. Become more aware of your body's natural rhythms. What time do you typically wake up (without the alarm)? What time are you *ready* to sleep? How do you feel with the amount of sleep you typically get? Make it a goal to go to bed early enough that you get the sleep you NEED in order to feel your best.

2. Be proactive and make time in each day to quiet your mind. Maybe just 60 seconds of closing your eyes and thinking positive, calming thoughts. There are apps that help you focus and calm your mind as well.

3. Spend time outside in nature. A 2019 study[18] of over 19,000 people showed that people who spend at least 2 hours in nature a week are significantly more likely to report good health and higher psychological wellbeing than those who don't visit nature at all during an average week. You can walk, hike, swim, bike, run, canoe, whatever....just be out in the natural world.

4. Let the things on the to-do list go unfinished once in a while. They can most likely wait, but your health cannot!

---

18   Nature: https://www.nature.com/articles/s41598-019-44097-3

*If I'm different from others,
I'm the one who needs to change.*

Truth:

You are just fine as you are.

Recently I've been looking through old photos. I suppose it's part of that "empty nest" thing.

I like to look at photos of my kids when they were little and marvel at how much time has passed. They were so cute with their little matching outfits at Easter (which they now love to tell me how much they HATED), their self-imposed haircuts, recital costumes, showing off their favorite Christmas toys, etc.

But OH MY GOSH what was wrong with ME?

I have several photos of my short haircut, circa 1998. That was not my best look. I was in graduate school and was just getting established in my job as a college teacher. All the women (it seemed) in my professional circles had short hair. It seemed to be the "professional look" for women. So, I had my hair cut.

I remember my daughters crying; they loved my below-the-shoulders hair.

Around that same time, I have photos of me in a denim dress. Now.... for those of you not old enough to remember, denim dresses were somewhat "in" at that time...at least for elementary school teachers and conservative church women.

Well, I *was* in a conservative church during that period of my life. Many of my friends were *teachers*.

I remember buying that darned dress. I thought "it's really not that attractive, but everyone is wearing them so I guess I should get one."

(Conversation with self upon viewing those photos: "Dang, woman. Those photos are NOT your best. Super short hair and a denim dress were NOT your style! What the heck were you thinking?")

I think I was trying to be someone else, to fit some mold that others had created. This is what a professional woman, a teacher, looks like.

Why did I feel the need to change who I was? Why did I think I needed to adapt myself, my style, my tastes... to fit in with those around me? Looking back, I realize I've been doing that all my life. I don't think I even KNEW what my own tastes and preferences were.

When I was a kid I tried to be like my brothers so they would like me (oh, I know now that they loved me, but older brothers probably never really *like* little sisters!). At school or church in those early years I was always trying to be like my buddies Debbie, Becky, and Linda. When I hung out with my very-tomboyish friend Lisa, I tried to be a tomboy. In high school, I wanted desperately to be like my friends Andrea and Stacey.

Around the time I turned 50 I began to see this pattern (yeah, I'm a little slow to notice patterns sometimes). I also began to feel more comfortable in my own skin and to realize that I don't need to change who I am.

I mean, we all have flaws and things we need to work on. I'm doing my best to work on those. But I'm no longer expending energy trying to "fit in." It's time to be real, to be me...to be the *real* me.

And guess what? I'm pretty fabulous just the way I am.

Golden nugget:

You are exactly what your world needs. Remember that old saying: The world would be pretty boring if we were all alike. It is true! So, no matter how you wear your hair or what your "style" is, rock it. Embrace it full force. The world needs the one-of-a-kind authentic YOU.

Exercise:

Think of something you have tried to change about yourself because you were trying to "fit in". Maybe it is your hair, your clothes, your music, your taste in food, a hobby (I that hear a lot of people take up golf just to impress a boss!). Write it in all caps (for example, "HAIR").

Then, write this sentence "My _____ is fabulous and I won't change it for anyone."

Read it *out loud* each morning. After a week, change the word; insert something else that you have tried to change. You are changing the message, and by reading it out loud, you are *hearing* the message. You can change how you think.

Lie:

I have to be available to everyone all the time.

Truth:

It's ok (and healthy) to set boundaries.

My office is on the 3rd floor in a 106 year-old building, the Conservatory of Music. It houses the music and theatre classes under the umbrella of the Department of Music and Theatre. One of my windows overlooks a big wooded area of campus; occasionally I look down and see deer frolicking on the grass.

In my humble opinion, I have the best colleagues in the world. They are literally some of the most wonderful and hard-working people I know. We are a tight-knit bunch. We have been through a lot together, both personally and professionally.

Our students are great too. Music students are extremely dedicated and hardworking. I can make this generalized comment because music majors typically take 18-19 credits (or more) per semester, due to all the ensembles and private lessons in their programs of study. You have to be or become organized and disciplined to remain a music major.

The Conservatory of Music, St. Mary-of-the-Woods College

I'm the Chairperson of the department which means, among other things, faculty and students come to me with questions or problems. That's not only a part of the job, but it is something I enjoy.

I like helping to solve problems and trying to figure out creative solutions.

Typically, I have an open door policy. I often have an open door, period. I usually close it only when I have a meeting or phone call, or really need to hunker down and get some project or report done.

I've noticed a pattern. I'm grooving along, making good progress on some report or preparing for a class, or grading papers. Suddenly I hear footsteps getting closer to my door (old wooden floors and all). I look up as someone knocks and peeks their head in.

"Gotta minute?"

I almost always say "yes" even if I really *cannot* spare a minute, let alone the five or ten minutes this matter will probably take.

One of my music business mentors, Amanda C. Williams, cautioned me about taking those "Gotta minute" meetings. They seem like no big deal…it's just a *minute*! But here's the problem: 1) they are never just 60 seconds, and 2) that "minute" interrupts the flow of what you are doing. Sometimes it takes quite a while to get your mind back in that flow after the "gotta minute" meeting is over.

But there's a third reason to not take them (unless it's an urgent matter that truly needs immediate attention).

When I take those meetings, I'm devaluing my own time, my own work. In a sense, I'm devaluing me. I cannot afford to do that. None of us can. But often, a "Superwoman" does not want to set those limits; we want to be helpful ...to a *fault*.

So I'm reconsidering my open door policy. I have not done anything drastic like posting a big orange neon sign saying NEVER COME IN THIS OFFICE WITHOUT AN APPOINTMENT... AND THAT MEANS YOU! I *am* thinking about how to set better limits. How to value my time and myself.

By the way, I'm not guiltless. I've done my share of requesting those "brief" meetings. I need to remember to do what I'm asking others to do. So, I'm working on not asking for "gotta minute" meetings from others. It starts with me.

Golden nugget:

Setting boundaries can be hard but it is often a means of *self-preservation*! **We deserve to preserve ourselves**. Our time is valuable. *We* are valuable.

Exercise:

Be honest....do you need better boundaries in some area of your life? Do some *free-flow writing*[19] on this topic. Set the timer for 5-10 minutes and just WRITE. No editing, no fixing. When the timer goes off read it out loud.

What needs to change in your life so that you are valuing yourSELF?

---

19   *Free-flow writing* is putting your pen to the paper and just writing non-stop for at least five minutes. Don't think, don't worry about neatness, don't stop to edit or censor or correct your spelling....just WRITE. Write your thoughts, feelings, fears, etc. on that topic. Don't let the pen leave the paper....keep writing until the timer goes off.

Lie:

Another life transition?
Bring it on...I can take it. No biggie.

Truth:

Yes you can. But don't fool yourself.
It's gonna be tough.

Here we go. This will be a tough one for me to write. And maybe a tough one for you to read, depending on how close it hits home for you. So feel free to take a break and/or grab a Kleenex if need be.

My baby is 18.

My daughters are 27 and 24. Don't get me wrong... it was hard when they left for college...very hard. But I always knew I had my "baby" at home. It made each of those transitions a little easier. Neither of their exits *changed my identity.* Now I'm an "empty nester."

He is a high school senior with his sights set on two things: 1) becoming a band director and 2) serving in the military. He is 6'4", a heck of a trumpet player, has a tender heart (especially for older folks and veterans), has a girlfriend, and makes average grades. He's a good kid…er…young man.

I forget sometimes that he is a young man. It's much easier for me to look at him and see the 4-year-old, trying to buy extra time to stay up on Christmas eve, who was on his way to his bedroom when he turned to me in all seriousness and said, "Oh and by the way…your Christmas tree is beautiful." Or who looked at a homemade stain glass project hanging in the window of his pre-school classroom and said, "It's *beautiful*… like a *girl*."

I don't know why certain memories stick in our minds. But those two really stick out to me. There are hundreds more, of course.

And he's leaving for college soon. Well, first he is going to be in a Drum Corps in Nashville all summer. Then he will start college.

Drum Corps is like professional marching band. It grew out of the military drum and bugle corps tradition and now consists of brass, percussion, and guard playing difficult music while performing an intricately choreographed show. They rehearse and tour the U.S. all summer until they compete in finals in August. I'm so proud of him for auditioning and getting accepted into this group.

He is passionate about Drum Corps. In his spare time, he watches videos of past performances. I have seen him cry only on rare occasions, and one of those occasions was during his high school years when I took him and some of his buddies to Drum Corps finals. A trumpet player played a super high note with perfect intonation. He had tears in his eyes.

What was I thinking in encouraging him to do Drum Corps…*this* summer? He'll be GONE all summer; then college will start! I mean… we could've done so many things together…go to the movies, hike at a state park, take a bunch of his friends and go to a water park…

Who am I kidding.

If he was home he might do those things, but probably not with mom. (He's not 10 anymore, Tracy!!)

So…this is a transition. Not only for me, but also for my husband. This is the last one to fly from the nest. When my oldest was born I was suddenly a mom. When the middle child came I became a referee. When my youngest leaves I will suddenly be the proverbial "empty nester."

And I cannot do my typical "No big deal...I've had lots of transitions....I can manage this one, no problem." That's my Superwoman façade. Deep down, I know this one is different. This is going to hurt. I'm going to miss him something terrible. I'm going to need my husband, my daughters, and my friends. I'm going to need my music.

Thank God for my support system and for the music. And yes...I'm already writing a song about this. I think maybe it will help me a little to start preparing myself for it now.

Transitions are hard especially when they have the potential to redefine you in some way.

Golden nugget:

Realize that you are going to need help through big life transitions, whatever those may be for you. Stay connected to your loved ones and to your music. You can't do it alone.

Exercise:

What transitions are on the horizon for you in the next 6 months? The next year? Write them here, along with friends and relatives who have faced something similar. Start a list of questions you might ask them (example below):

Transition Topic	Who has gone through it	Questions I have	Support System
Empty nest	Lots of people! Leslie, Mara, April, Karla, Julie	What does it feel like? How did you cope with this new reality? Did you take up new hobbies? How long did it "sting?"	Husband, daughters, friends
Becoming an author	Bill R., John O., Sharon B.	Did you get a publisher or self-publish? How did you promote it?	Sharon, Katie, Sherry, Beth

*There is nothing special about me;
anyone can do what I do.*

Truth:

*You have unique talents and skills...
it's time to acknowledge them!*

The Shield

Every superwoman has a shield as part of her superhero attire. How do I know this? Just try giving a superwoman a compliment. She will deflect it. She will tell you it was no big deal, or that she did not accomplish it alone. She will "poo poo" it!

I'm guilty of this too. In part, it is how I was raised. My mom set the example. She was always quiet and humble about her talents and always acknowledged others for their contributions. She deflected a lot.

She is an amazing artist and people tell her that all the time. She says "thank you" but typically follows that with a statement about how it could've been better if she'd had more time, or if she'd used a different shade of green, or how it's "just an old barn and windmill" or something like that. I mean...her stuff is amazing but she just doesn't see it as *special*. She has an innate talent and has also worked at her craft for many years. But still she doesn't see her art as really anything outstanding or remarkable.

Recently I was complimented a couple of times regarding an academic program I created. It's a unique program that has been really successful for our college, and it took over 10 years of developing, refining, and advocating (and perseverance) on my part to make it happen.

Both times instead of simply saying "Thank you" I said "Thank you, but..." as I went on to acknowledge others who have helped the program grow and thrive.

Of course, it's ok to share the love and share credit where it is due. That is the right thing to do. But first I need to learn to just say "Thank you." Because I DID do a lot. Not everyone would have had the perseverance to do what I did, or the knowledge of how academic programs work, or the passion for creating something that would help people achieve their dreams. That particular "recipe" of qualities and knowledge is something that resides within me.

It is not a bad thing to acknowledge ourselves for what we bring to the table. It's not undue pride or arrogance to say "I created this thing and it was good" or "I had a great idea and took the steps to make it happen" or "I have this talent or drive that not everyone has."

Golden Nugget:

Let's put down our shields, stop deflecting, and say "thank you." Let's accept that we just might have something special about us. It is not arrogance.

Exercise:

In what situations do you tend to deflect compliments? Can you simply say "thank you"?

Practice it in the mirror. Compliment yourself for something (out loud), then give a reply. For example, I might look in the mirror and say "Tracy you did a great job on that report", and then I would look myself in the eyes and say "Thank you!" And mean it!

I need to be productive 24/7.

Some days you just need to be a sloth.[20]

Today was one of those days. I guess I just needed to be a sloth.

Well, I started out as usual; not "slothy" at all. It's Saturday but I had a recruiting event at work, then a music contest for my son, all before 11:00am. So, I was up at 6, took my walk, did my yoga/stretching, ate breakfast, and hit the shower. I did my recruiting thing then heard my son perform and was home by noon.

I thought "This is great! I have the rest of the day. I can get so much done!" I ate lunch. Then I crashed.

---

20   No offense meant to any real-life sloths!

I literally collapsed on the couch and went sound asleep. I think a nuclear blast could've happened and I wouldn't have budged. It's bitter cold outside and I had the fireplace going. It was so ...darn...comfy.

When I woke up an hour later I felt better but exhausted at the same time. I could not get up or get motivated to do anything. I had a whole list of things I wanted to accomplish today. Eventually I did get off the couch, and got some things done... but not nearly as much as I should have.

Did you catch that word "should?" I'm judging myself. When I'm not *productive* I often hear my Dad's voice saying "you need to get busy!" He had a VERY strong work ethic which I learned from him. And it has served me well for the most part. But if I'm not staying busy I can get very judgmental toward myself.

I think judging ourselves is another common trait among superwomen. There usually IS something else to be done, so we never feel we've done *enough*.

I am a planner, a list maker. Typically, when I take my morning walk I'm planning out my day. I'm making mental notes, and when I get back to the house I fill up a post-it note that I then put on my laptop. I add stuff to my Outlook calendar. Even on the weekend I still make lists of the things I can't squeeze onto my Monday-Friday post-it notes.

But today my body and mind must have needed a break. And I am learning that it's ok to take that break. I don't want to form a habit of it; I mean, I can't afford to crash every Saturday (or can I?). But I *can* go easy on myself when I have an occasional Sloth Day Maybe it should be a monthly holiday? Then I could put it in my planner!

Golden nugget:

When you try SO hard to be Superwoman, your body *will...push... back*. Guaranteed. Listen to your body. Take care of it. And know that is necessary to be a sloth once in a while.

Exercise:

Write a letter from your Body to You. What would your body say to you? What does it need?

Lie:

I don't need to focus on me;
that can wait.

Truth:

Tomorrow is not guaranteed.

Recently a woman in our songwriting community passed unexpectedly. She was only a few years older than me; she was much too young to go.

She was a vibrant, warm, sweet, empathic, beautiful human being. When I talked to her, I always knew she was really, deeply listening. She was an encourager, always telling others in the community what was great about their music. I never heard her say a negative thing.

And I don't understand how this could happen to her so suddenly. Just this past summer at our songwriting conference, she was fully alive, laughing, smiling, writing, singing her heart out. Never in a million years would I have thought this could happen.

It's made me stop and think (as death often does)…

What do I want to accomplish here? What if I don't have tomorrow? If it is possible to have any regrets on "the other side," what will I regret not having done? What will I regret not having said?

I don't have a big, brilliant revelation, but I'm thinking about this a lot.

We hear these sayings all the time: "Live life to the fullest!", "You only have one life!", "Follow your dream!" I'm afraid they have become clichés to us. We don't think about the underlying reality which is *you may not have any more tomorrows.*

As a recovering Superwoman I can relate to putting others first much of the time. Many times it is by necessity. I mean, I'm a mom. Once you are in the parenting role, it's not all about you anymore. There are others to consider, others who depend on you.

But two of my kids are now fully adults, and one is an adult "in training." So there is a bit more time to figure out how I want to spend my time and what I want to accomplish here.

At this moment, this is what's on my mind:

- I want to write songs. A lot of songs. I want to perform them and see/hear how people respond. I want my songs to *move* people to *feel* something they needed to feel. I want to record, to become a better musician, to write with others, to continue learning about the music business. I want to employ my music for good purposes.
- I want to travel and see more of the U.S and the world.
- I want to be a positive force in this world. I want to act and speak with kindness, compassion, empathy, and forgiveness.
- I want to laugh with friends and family, and to deepen those connections.

So… I don't have a "bucket list" as some people talk about. But I do want to be working everyday toward the above "goals". I've made my list for today. It includes a lot of writing and practicing. And maybe I'll start thinking about a trip with my girlfriends.

Golden Nugget:

Take advantage of today. Think about what you want to accomplish in this life. And in the words of the song by Tim Nichols and Craig Wiseman, "Live Like You Were Dying."

Exercise:

Alright, I'm caving in. I am finally going to make a bucket list. Things I want to do before I "kick the bucket." I encourage you to do it too. Maybe start with just 2-3 BIG things you'd like to do.

Guess what...there is an app for that! Here is the website: https://bucketlist.org

On their website they ask you to set goals and enter a DATE for each goal. That is very smart. They even state that a "goal without a target date is a dream."

Or you can write it on a sticky note and put it on your mirror: Write a specific goal and a specific date by which you will accomplish it. Read it out loud each day: "I will travel to Greece by September 1, 2023" There....I've written one!! Your turn!

Santorini island, Greece. ABSFreePic.com

Lie:

I need to be on the same path as the women I admire.

Truth:

Your path is unique and is just right for you.

As soon as I typed the word "path" above I thought immediately of the Robert Frost poem, "The Road Not Taken." You know the one…it says when a road splits and becomes two roads, you have to go one way or the other. You can't take both roads. You have to make a choice. And even if you come back and try to take the other road later on, it's not the same road it was. Time has passed. That road has changed from what it once was. And *you* are different too.

There is so much to unpack in that poem!

But for now, I'm focusing on the fact that sometimes I am envious of the "path" other women have taken. I see something in them that I admire and I get a little jealous. I admit it.

Ok, I'll address the obvious ones first. I envy women who are successful singer-songwriters and/or performers. Carole King, Lucinda Williams, Dolly Parton, Mary Chapin Carpenter, Lori McKenna, etc., etc. I look at them and think "Where might I be if I had moved to Nashville and put all my music chips on the table? Where would I be if I'd taken their paths?" They seem to have it all.

Then there are my female friends and acquaintances who are very much in the local limelight. They are in a variety of high profile professions such as doctor, business owner, executive director, CEO, etc. They seem to have "made it." They seem happy, energized, passionate about their work and, to be honest, they seem very well-off financially.

Hmmm....they all "seem" to be a lot of things.

How do I *know* they "have it all", or that they are happy, energized, etc.? Can I determine their happiness by the fact that they had x number of hit songs/records? Or, in the case of my friends, what can I really determine from Facebook? After all, we all put our best selves forward on social media most of the time, so it's easy to look at others and think "they've got it all".

I have read about some of the personal heartaches and struggles of my singer-songwriter and performer idols. Carole King went through several marriages including an abusive relationship. Lori McKenna lost her mom when she was only 7 years old. Dolly Parton grew up dirt poor and had to struggle to assert herself in a male-dominated music business. I don't envy those struggles. Not one bit. I don't envy what they may have had to sacrifice (especially privacy) to be where they are today.

It is so easy to look at others and only see the shiny and sparkly aspects of their lives. The number of hit songs they've written, the traveling, the wide smiles on their websites, the apparent financial success. It's easy to constantly question "am I on the right path?", "should I have gone that direction?"

The ironic thing is that I suspect that there just might be some women who have these same thoughts about me (and you). They might look at what we post on Facebook and say "She seems to have it made." Maybe they see that I am a professor and think "If only I had gone that route I could have had so much respect or opportunity."

So, my big "aha" for today is that I am on the particular path I am on for some reason. I need to be here. There's a lot to do on this path and I am actually changing it every day as I walk on it. I've widened it a bit and I've noticed little side roads I wanted to explore.

Mr. Frost didn't talk about that option...widening the path, and making it include other things that were not originally on the path.

Maybe he never met a superwoman!

Golden Nugget:

Even in the midst of all the stuff we are juggling even a superwoman can get a little envious. Let's try to recognize that and then set it aside. Let's honor our own unique path and look for ways to widen it.

Exercise:

Grab some art supplies; they don't have to be fancy. Maybe crayons and construction paper. Or if you want a treat, go get some oil pastels[21] and heavy drawing paper (as long as you are treating yourself get a big size of paper, like 12 x 18). Just know that your artistic skills do NOT matter in this exercise.

Now draw a simple path across that paper. Maybe it's just a straight line, or maybe its curvy and goes up and down some hills you draw. Imagine one end of the path represents your past, and the other is your future.

Draw a stick figure of yourself walking the path...somewhere in between the two "points" mentioned above. On the part of the path that lies behind you, draw or list some things in your past that have led to who you are today. Parents, school, relationships, jobs, passions, children,

---

21   Oil pastels can be a little messy, so cover your workspace with newspaper or an old sheet. The fun thing is that oil pastels can be smudged and blended with your fingers which makes you feel more creative and artistic! Spray your artwork with a fixative spray when you are finished.

etc. On the path in front of you list some things you want to have on your path in the future. Make the path a little wider. Draw some side roads you may want to explore. Keep working on it until it is a picture you like.

Two roads diverged in a yellow wood,
And sorry I could not travel both
And be one traveler, long I stood
And looked down one as far as I could
To where it bent in the undergrowth;

Then took the other, as just as fair,
And having perhaps the better claim,
Because it was grassy and wanted wear;
Though as for that the passing there
Had worn them really about the same,

And both that morning equally lay
In leaves no step had trodden black.
Oh, I kept the first for another day!
Yet knowing how way leads on to way,
I doubted if I should ever come back.

I shall be telling this with a sigh
Somewhere ages and ages hence:
Two roads diverged in a wood, and I—
I took the one less traveled by,
And that has made all the difference.
- Robert Frost[22]

---

22   The Road Not Taken, Robert Frost, 1916

ie:

*I'm always busy,
but I'm not accomplishing anything.*

Truth:

*You are accomplishing important
things everyday.*

Today is Groundhog Day. I don't know about you but the movie by that title is one of my favorites. Every time I hear Sonny and Cher's "I Got You Babe" I laugh as I recall Bill Murray waking up to that song every morning (well, technically, it was the *same* morning over and over) until he finally smashes the clock radio.

I feel that way some days…like I'm waking up to the same crazy day I've woken up to 10,000 times before. I feel like going back to sleep, or smashing the alarm clock (well, technically, my phone is my "clock" these days).

But instead, I start my daily routine… again.

‖: Get out of bed. Get dressed, talk a walk, breakfast, brush my teeth, get ready, let the dog out, go to work, do a bunch of stuff, go home, fix dinner, eat dinner, clean up dinner, do laundry, go to bed :‖ (Hopefully the musicians will understand the funny marks as repeat signs...)

What the heck did I accomplish today anyway??

Superwomen have this tendency to think they have to be doing BIG, obvious, things. Things that make the front page of the newspaper (or at least things we are proud enough to "post" about on Facebook). Things our mothers might brag about. If we are not accomplishing something big, we sometimes feel like we have failed. It's "all or nothing." I accomplish something huge or nothing that I do matters.

Why am I not further in my career? Why is it taking so long to achieve my fitness goals? Will I ever get "there"?

Can we take a minute to recognize that the little things matter? And to acknowledge that where we are right this minute matters?

If we are honest, we are (most days) working toward *something*. Even if it's "just" working toward the next paycheck...that matters. It's no small thing when it comes to feeding your babies and paying the mortgage. Even if we are standing in an unemployment line, we are doing something. If I'm blogging about something I care about, or simply listening to someone who needs a friendly ear, does that matter? Is it "big" enough?

Can we take a minute to recognize that *we matter*? That our existence, no matter how routine and *seemingly* insignificant, changes the world? (By the way...NO one's existence is insignificant).

This reminds me of the *butterfly effect*[23]. In pop culture, there is this belief that something as small as the flutter of a butterfly's wings can cause a tornado half way around the world. You might remember Jeff Goldblum's character in Jurassic Park talking about this theory. I like

---

23   Butterfly Effect: I did a little digging and the actual butterfly theory is different than the popular version. It came from a scientist names Edward Lorenz. It states that some complex systems (like weather) are very unpredictable so their outcome can be greatly changed by small variances. https://www.americanscientist.org/article/understanding-the-butterfly-effect

this idea and I think there is a bit of truth to it.

I don't think I'm begin too dramatic here. The smile I offered my co-worker as she passed me in the hall could change how she is thinking about herself today. And it could put other positive things into action.

Because I did laundry last night my son was able to wear his favorite shirt today which makes him feel more confident and positive, which changes his day, which could change the day of those around him.

The little song I wrote and shared with my friend lifted her out of the dark mood she was in, which allowed her to call her mom and be positive, which spurred her mom to take dinner to a family who had just been through a funeral.

I read a story once about a prison psychologist who did an IQ test on an inmate. Long story short, many years later the ex-inmate ran into the psychologist (who didn't even remember the former inmate); the man told the psychologist "You changed my life with five words. You told me 'You have a high IQ' and no one had ever told me that. It made me begin to see myself differently and to work toward a new life, which I now have achieved."

Wow. What a huge difference 5 little words made.

You need to understand that by going through your daily routine, doing "little" things, you ARE accomplishing things. You may never know how important those things are. You may never see the "tornado" that occurs because you spread your wings and flew a little bit.

So go on....fly!

Golden Nugget:

Let's change our self-talk. Let's focus on what we ARE accomplishing and start telling ourselves that our "little" lives matter, even when we are just going through the routine.

PS: Oh, and confession time. Although I *started* this page on Groundhog's day, I'm *finishing* it a week later. I've been berating myself for not getting it done earlier. I'm trying to take my own advice and realize I've accomplished a lot of little things in the last week. Geez.

Exercise:

List one positive thing you did today that seems minor (for example, washed dishes or drove to work). Now list 3-5 positive things that could *potentially* result from that ONE thing. For example:

- Minor thing: I drove to work
- Potential positive result (PPR): I made money for my survival; I went to a meeting and gave an idea that may help our company; I wrote an encouraging note to a co-worker who was discouraged.

Each one of those PPRs could have 3-5 additional PPRs! Those little things you accomplished have a way of spreading.

*If I were younger/thinner/more attractive
I'd be happy.*

You've got to change your self-talk.

Ok this is where it gets real....

I was at a songwriters' festival recently; what a great experience. In the span of a few days you can go to several venues across the city and hear the most wonderful songwriters! Some of them have top ten hits on the radio now, and some had hits years ago. It's wonderful to get to hear the original songwriter sing the song the way they imagined it.

At one show, there were two men and two women on stage in the round (a "round" is where one person sings a song, then the next, and when they've all sung once, that's one "round". Then they keep doing rounds until time is up). They were all young, attractive people from my point of view…mid 20s to late 30s in my estimation.

The first thing one of the women said before she played was in reference to how old she was compared to the other songwriters on the stage. She said something to the effect of "You know, I'm in my 40s and I'm obviously the oldest one on stage, so don't look very closely or you'll see all my wrinkles."

What??!

I immediately looked around the crowd. At least ¼ of the audience was made up of people easily over 40. Women in their 50s (including me), 60s, and maybe 70s. Women with gray hair and wrinkles. I wondered how they felt about that comment.

I thought to myself, why did she start with that statement? First of all, she was beautiful! Second of all, this was not a beauty competition; people came to hear her because they love her songs. Her looks have nothing to do with the quality of her songs. Heck, a lot of songwriters don't even have great voices, but she had that going for her too!

I'm not faulting her. She was simply repeating the message she hears/ sees hundreds of times a day on social media, billboards, TV, and in magazines. It is pervasive and relentless and downright dangerous.

I'm tired of hearing women (myself included) put themselves down for their weight, their looks, their age, and on and on. I'm really, really tired of it.

Where do we get this twisted message? The message that we are all supposed to look a certain way. The message that a woman who is over 30 (or even over 60!) is not attractive. The message that a woman who is a bit larger at 40 than she was at 20 is "too big." Again, a lot of this comes from media messages and the fact that, as a society, we have *normalized* and *internalized* those messages.

Such messages are one reason we still love sun tanned skin even when we know that tanning in the sun is not safe. In the 1920s it became fashionable to have tanned skin; it represented health and pleasure[24]. Now, even though we know sun tanning is dangerous, it is hard to change

---

24   Tanning: https://www.skincancer.org/prevention/tanning/tale-of-tanning

our behavior and what we think is attractive, because for *100 years* we have valued tanned skin as healthy and "glowing."

In America, we become obsessed with what we see and hear in the media. It becomes reality to us, even though it's not. Most women do not look like Kate Upton or Jennifer Lopez or Beyoncé.

Another good example of media distortion is thinness as an ideal for females. This internalized ideal has tortured countless girls and women since at least the 1960s. That's when Twiggy emerged as the "in" model of the day. Her name describes her appearance; she was ultra-thin and her look became fashionable and desirable (which is interesting and ironic given that Marilyn Monroe and Jane Mansfield, both very curvy women, were the "desirable" types just a few years prior to Twiggy's emergence!).

This relatively new cultural phenomenon of "thin is in" got serious very quickly; by the 1970s there were many documented cases of eating disorders, notably anorexia and bulimia, mostly occurring in girls and women. In 1980 the DSM-III (Diagnostic and Statistical Manual for Mental Disorders) included eating disorders for the first time. In 1983 Karen Carpenter died from complications of a heart weakened by anorexia at a time when the world really still didn't even know about those conditions.

Of course that idea...the worshipping of thinness....has fueled the multi-billion dollar diet industry too. That is another reason thinness continues to be promoted; it's good business for the dieting industry.

I grew up in that era of the 70s and 80s. I remember what it felt like to be a girl at that time...to constantly be judged and to judge myself. The pressure, the horrible self-talk when I ate "too much" or didn't look the way I wanted to in my jeans or a swimsuit. The avoidance of shopping for clothes. The drive to always be not just "thin" but "thinner."

It has taken a lot of years, and some really good therapy, for me to develop more positive self-messages. And those negative cultural messages are even MORE pervasive now with the rise of social media.

(Sidebar: We all do the self-talk thing, and many times the messages we give ourselves are messages we heard from parents, society, or others. Self-talk affects how we feel about ourselves and how we act, so if you are not aware of your self-talk messages I encourage you to think about it. Change the message. Use your self-talk to give yourself positive messages).

Should we strive to be healthy?? Absolutely. But thin doesn't always equal healthy.

(By the way...lots of boys and men suffer from eating disorders too. And positive self-talk is not just for females.)

So, if I had the opportunity to have coffee with that 40+ year-old fabulous female songwriter, what would I want to say?

I think I would say "I love your songs; you have such a gift and I thank you for sharing that gift with the world. And I have a wish for you... my wish for you is that you can begin to accept yourself for the wonderful person that you are, the fabulous and skilled songwriter that you are.... and that you will focus on what is real and important about you, and not buy into society's twisted messages. You are amazing!"

Please excuse me for a minute while I go to the mirror and practice what I've been preaching.

Golden Nugget:

Being younger, or thinner, or whatever is not going to lead to happiness. To be happy we have to start by being content with who we are *right in this very moment*, and THAT starts with how we think about ourselves. Let's try to be aware of the messages being "fed" to us by society, and those that we feed to ourselves. When a negative message emerges, change the channel... start filling your brain with positive self-talk. Go ahead...start now.

Exercise:

In the space below (or on a bigger sheet of paper, if need be)
- What is that <u>one thing</u> you think would make you happy? Money? Being thinner? Having fewer wrinkles? Write it down.

_____

- Write down the things you DO have in your life that make you happy...kids, best friend, sunrise, fresh flowers, favorite song, favorite food, etc. Write as many as you can. Rate your happiness 0 (none) to 10 (overwhelming) on each item. Post it on your bathroom mirror and read it out loud each morning and night.

My "happies"	0-10

- What are some of the negative messages you tell yourself?
  - When you become aware of one, write it down.
  - Write down where it came from (did you hear it from a parent?) When do you remember first hearing/saying that message?
  - Write down a counter-attack message for each negative message. How can you fight that negative message? Write down the thing that a person who loves you unconditionally would say to you. For example, if you find yourself thinking "I am so fat", you might develop a counter message that goes something like: "No. I am not fat. I am a wonderful person. If I need to lose some weight for my health, ok, I'll work on that. But my weight does not define me. I am not "fat"...I'm a perfect-as-I-am, lovable human being."
  - Work on saying those messages out loud EVERY time the negative one appears in your mind. Look yourself in the mirror and say the positive message. Believe it. It won't feel authentic for some time. Just keep doing it.

Negative messages	Counter attack/ Positive messages

Lie:

I'm stuck with a life I'm not excited about.

Truth:

Create your ideal life.

When I was getting my master's degree in counseling we had to study a lot of counseling theories. Theories by Freud, Adler, Rogers, Bandura, Beck, Yalom, etc. Each one focuses on different ideas regarding what causes our interpersonal problems and how to solve them. We were challenged to figure out which theory (or theories) fit us best; which ones would guide our work as helping professionals.

If you've ever read about those differing theories and the people who developed them you know the theories tend to stem from how the theorist viewed the world. Each theory tends to be a reflection of that person's personality and experiences.

I discovered some truth in each one of those theories, although I can say that the behavioral approaches to counseling and therapy have always felt a bit stilted and sometimes "robotic" to me. There is a place for it, and it sometimes works. I gravitate toward the more person-centered approaches. What does the person in front of me need *right now*? What is practical for them? How can I help them learn how to meet their own needs?

Well... in all of this studying of theories, I got to thinking about creativity. It is essential in my life. I feel best when I am creating something. For me it is usually creating music. But I also get energized by creating new ways of doing things that solve some problem; for example, creating new academic programs for the college where I work.

I started noticing that most people have some sort of creative "outlet", typically relegated to a hobby of some sort. Cooking, woodworking, painting, sewing, dancing, blogging, singing, playing an instrument, gardening, grand parenting, etc.

I thought "Why do so many people create things? Why does it seem that we have a need to create?"

Then I thought about God/The Divine/The Creator. If you are not "religious", please don't stop reading. I certainly don't have the same concept of God now as I did back when I "created" this theory (which, I've discovered, has been voiced by others before me).

This is what I think: I think there is some mysterious Divine force. Call it God, Great Spirit, Universe, Trinity, Goddess, Buddha, or whatever you conceptualize it to be. It is the original Creative Force in this universe. And somehow, we came from that creative force; therefore, we have creativity in our DNA. We must create. We are happiest and most fulfilled when we are creating.

If you are familiar with Christian teachings you might know that the Bible states we are "made in God's image." To me, that means we are creative forces because "God" is the original Creative Force. Therefore, we *need* to create in order to feel fulfilled.

When you are doing what you love to do (often something creative), you sometimes even lose track of time (that's a concept called *Flow*[25] which is being researched quite extensively). When we create, we are pouring ourselves into something/someone but we are filled up in the process. Pouring yourself out through your creativity fills some hole in the world; but you are also being replenished by doing that thing. It's weird how that works! I pour myself out but I am refilled in the process. Damn… that's good stuff!

Why the departure into this theory on creativity, Tracy?, you might be asking yourself.

Well I hope it's evident. **Music** is my creative force. It has been there from the time I was at least 3. It is the thing that makes me happiest. It makes me lose track of time and it blocks out everything else, demands my entire focus, brings me intense joy and profound sorrow, soothes me, heals me, turns me on a dime. And when I engage in music, especially in songwriting, I am tapping into my creativity in a way that *demands* I pour myself out; but at the same time, it fills me up.

You have this creative capacity and need, too. Maybe it is something else for you. Maybe it is cooking, or making up new recipes, or painting the barn, or sewing for your grandkids, or working on the engine of the car you are restoring, or coaching a team, or making games for your kids, etc.

Whatever it is that fires you up…just do it.

Golden Nugget:

Bottom line…when you engage your creativity, you create yourself. You create your own happiness, your reason to be. It is not selfish; it is essential.

Exercise:

Do you already know what your creative love is? If so, take a few minutes today to DO it or to make a plan to do it within the next week

---

25   Csikszentmihalyi's Flow theory: https://study.com/academy/lesson/mihaly-csikszentmihalyi-flow-theory-works.html

(and write down your target date on your calendar or planner to hold yourself accountable).

Don't know what your creative self loves to do? Spend a few minutes writing about things you have always wanted to try but have not done. Free write (no editing as you go). Set the timer for 5-10 minutes and stop when it dings. Read what you wrote and circle any word or activity that indicates being creative in any way.

If there is nothing in your list that you are just dying to do, repeat the writing exercise tomorrow. Keep doing it until something pops out at you as your "HECK YES, I MUST DO THIS."

Doing what I love, 2019

Lie:

I'm too old to _____.

Truth:

In the words of Nike, Just Do It.

I just got my monthly AARP magazine in the mail (sidebar: My husband is 5 years older than me. When he got his first AARP card, I jokingly told him I could not be seen with him any longer because he was old. He said "Well ok, but I get discounts." I said "Oh ok, I was just kidding!")

There is a great story in this issue of AARP. In fact, there are almost always some very inspirational stories about what people are doing in their "later" years. The one this month is about Kathie Lee Gifford.

In the article Kathie Lee talks about pursuing her dream job. It seems that even though she has been a very successful talk show host for many years, that path was always her *plan B*. She always wanted to act and sing. So now, at 65, she is walking away from a great paying gig at NBC to pursue the thing she has wanted since she was a little girl.

This inspires me. She is (pardon me, Kathie Lee) a *senior citizen*, and she is diving into a new career, diving into the thing she has always wanted to do but has not fully done. She is taking a chance, going for broke, leaving nothing on the table.

We can make excuses all day about why it may work for her and not us ("She's already well known", "She has money to spare", "She still looks great", etc.). **Why do we sell out before we even try? Who gets to decide when you are *too old* to do something?**

In fact, women are only the "right age" for about 2 minutes of their lives around their 30th birthday.

Ok, I'm exaggerating…a little. Depending on the industry a woman is in, she *may* have a few years of being viewed as old enough to have the experience she needs and young enough to still pursue her desired path. Maybe.

But in many industries she is never the "right age." She goes from being too young to be promoted or taken seriously to instantly being "post-career" age (typically the minute she has a baby).

This phenomenon is called *age-related bias*[26] and it commonly intersects with gender. Women are often seen as simultaneously too young <u>and</u> too old. Talk about odds being stacked against you!

Social norms dictate much of this thinking. Women are expected to fulfill certain roles, and those roles occur at certain times. For example: a woman in her 20s may apply for a leadership position and is thought to not have enough experience to hold that position. So she applies again in her early-mid 30's (still without children); the interviewer may think to themselves "I wonder how soon she will have a child and how that will affect her performance in this position."

A woman who HAS children may be questioned about how she will

---

26   Age related bias: www.theglobeandmail.com/report-on-business/careers/career-advice/life-at-work/too-young-too-old-but-never-the-right-age/article4394827/

handle a sick child on the day of a big meeting (whereas, let's be real...a man would likely not be asked this question). A woman in her 50s or 60s who decides to go back to graduate school or start a new business may "cause" some to wonder why she is "starting over" so late in life, or why she is not spending those years with her grandchildren.

What do you think you are too old to do? Travel? Get married again? Start a successful business? Go back to school? Write a hit song? Run your own art studio? Run for office?

What is holding you back? Don't make assumptions about what the future holds. If you want it, go for it.

Golden Nugget:

No matter how old you are, you are not cast in stone. You can evolve. Doesn't that make life more exciting to know we are not limited in how many times we can invent ourselves, or how many years it takes for us to get to the point where we are ready to chase that big dream? We can do what we want. We do not need to buy into society's ideas about what we "should" be doing based on our age.

Exercises:

1. Make a list of everything you are too *young* to do. You heard me. What are you too young for? I'll give you a few from my list:
   a. I'm too young to sit in a rocking chair all day
   b. I'm too young to eat pureed food
   c. I'm too young to stop traveling
   d. I'm too young to stop caring what my hair looks like
   Make a list of at least 20 things (ok, you can borrow a couple of mine if you like).

   Now...after each item, list what you *want* to do. Maybe it is the opposite of that other item. Play with it. See what comes up. Don't overthink it! **Do it quickly**.
   a. I'm too young to sit in a rocking chair all day, so I'm going hiking.

b. I'm too young to eat pureed food, so I'm going to treat myself to a nice steak.

c. I'm too young to stop traveling, so I'm going to look for a travel deal to a place I've always wanted to go... maybe Greece!

d. I'm too young to stop caring what my hair looks like, so I think I'll play with a new color or style.

Just do it.

Lie:

I need to speak/act/look "like a lady."

Truth:

Be the real YOU.

"That skirt is too short; you look like a slut."

Ouch.

That's what a boyfriend said to me....many years ago.

I had worn a very cute mini-skirt that had taken considerable courage to buy, and even more courage to wear, due to my severe body insecurities. He was fully aware of those insecurities. In one sentence, he shamed me and destroyed any confidence I had.

• • • • •

"That shirt is cut too low."

"Don't sit with your legs sprawled apart; it's not ladylike."

"Don't say what you really think; it might offend someone."

"Don't be so loud and bossy; people will think you're a bitch."

"You can have it all; just go for it."

These are just a few things girls hear as they grow up. I'm not blaming only males for saying these things; in fact, I remember sometimes thinking similar thoughts about other women. I remember even imparting some version of these messages to my own daughters. Shame on me.

These "rules for girls" are everywhere! On TV, in magazines, in conversations, in school and church. We hear and see those messages so frequently they become normal and are *fully engrained in us.* We often don't even question them. We believe them. We think and say them not only to ourselves but to other girls and women.

We learn early on there are *norms* that must be followed if we want to be accepted. So... we learn to try to fit the acceptable, cultural mold for women.

What is wrong with just being fully who we ARE? With wearing and saying what we WANT? Nothing. But society does a great job of making us THINK there is something wrong with it...something wrong with us.

We *all* have the right to be who we are....to say what we want....to dress how we like.

Why is it especially important for girls and women to feel empowered to fully embrace and celebrate who they are? Because from an early age girls are put under a microscope. Girls are celebrated for their looks and behavior over their interests and accomplishments.

Girls learn very early that there are ways to act that are unladylike, such as being bossy, or demanding, or wearing a shirt cut too low, and they are taught to not do those things. It all gets engrained in our brains and makes for deep insecurities and a feeling that there are definite rules to be followed.

We don't know even who we are because we are always trying to fit some preconceived mold of who we think we *should* be.

We internalize all the rules that society has for girls, such as, "you need to look a certain way", "don't speak your true opinion", "don't disagree with a boy you might like."

I am so proud of my daughters. They have developed strong, authentic voices. One of them spoke up to a football player in high school. He said to her (in front of the class) "You cross country runners aren't *real* athletes, like us football players." She replied "How many miles did YOU run today? I ran seven. And when did your team last win a state championship? Oh, that's right, you haven't won any, but my team has won several."

My other daughter wrote and performs a one-woman play that shines a light on women of Celtic history. One of them, Maeve, was married off to a brutal king (along with her sisters) when she was very young. She is often described in historical accounts, written by men, simply as "promiscuous" when she was in fact, a smart, cunning, and bold woman who became a powerful queen.

My daughters are bold and brave women; they are teaching *me* to be bold, be who I am, and to say what I need to say.

I wonder....what would I say if someone told me today that my "skirt was too short" or my shirt was "cut too low" or that I was being "too loud and bossy"? Hmm. Part of me would want to say things I cannot write here without them being edited out. I might say "I can't control what you or anyone thinks about me. All I can do is be who *I* am...be true to me. And I like me just as I am."

Golden nugget:

We all have internalized some unhealthy messages over time. It is time to recognize how they have shaped us, to reject them, and to replace them with healthier options. It is our right as humans to live authentically!

Exercise:

What are some messages you have heard from someone, or from magazines or TV, etc. about how you "should" look, or speak, or act? Do you remember times in your life when you were told to dress differently or speak more softly or act a certain way?

Draw a stick figure of you (no art skills required here, just a basic stick figure!) holding a BIG shield in each hand. Draw some arrows coming toward you and on each one, write one of the unhealthy messages you heard. On each shield, write healthy messages to block/counter those arrows.

Notice on the example below that the last part of each "Healthy message" is the same. Think about that phrase.

Unhealthy Message on arrow	Healthy Message on shield
That shirt is cut too low	I'll be the judge of that and will wear what I feel confident in. Whatever anyone else thinks of it is not within my power to control.
Don't sit with your legs sprawled apart	I'll sit how it feels most comfortable for me. Whatever anyone else thinks of it is not within my power to control.
Don't say what you really think	I will say what I think because it is my truth; I need to speak, and the world needs to hear, my truth. Whatever anyone else thinks of it is not within my power to control.
Don't be loud and bossy	I will be loud and bossy when I feel it is needed. Whatever anyone else thinks of it is not within my power to control.

About the Author

Dr. Tracy Richardson is a Professor of Music Therapy and the Chairperson of the Music and Theatre Department at Saint Mary-of-the-Woods College (SMWC), and has taught at SMWC since 1995. Dr. Richardson is a board-certified music therapist with a doctorate in Counselor Education. She has worked with people with a variety of mental and physical health issues. She specializes in the use of clinical songwriting as a music therapy intervention and teaches other music therapists how to use clinical songwriting. In addition to her work at SMWC she has a part-time music therapy practice and consults with companies on teambuilding through music.

Tracy Richardson is a singer/songwriter and keyboard player with three CDs to her credit. She has performed in bands and solo for over 30 years, opening for acts such as George Strait, John Conlee, Randy Travis, Keith Whitley, and Earl Thomas Conley. One of her original songs, *In Parke County,* received radio airplay, while her *Wabash River Song* was placed on the TV show Gear Heads (MavTV). She is a member of the Nashville Songwriters Association International (NSAI) and Songpreneurs (a Nashville-based songwriting community led by Grammy-award winning songwriter, Amanda Colleen Williams). Tracy continues to write, record, and perform regularly.

"Who Moved My Cape?!" is Tracy's first book and was written as a companion project to her 2019 CD project, "Superwoman Blues." You can find out more about her projects at www.TracyRichardsonMusic.com and find her music at iTunes, GooglePlay, Amazon, and other sites. Follow Tracy Richardson Music on Facebook.

Tracy is married to George and has three grown and fabulous children.